the birds fly

poems

For Maureen
Happy 85th !! :-
♡ Dayna

Dayna E. Mazzuca

Library & Archives Canada ISBN
978-0-9950108-7-1

KDP ISBN
9781790827596

Contact Author: 2dayna@telus.net
www.daynawrites.com

The Lord bless you and make his face

shine upon you...

Numbers 6: 22-27

CONTENTS

rain

let the rain fall

mute the commercials,

peel back labels, paper leaves —

eat whole foods; unfriend the world

wonder at the effect   silence has

                                    in solitude

…and then

time, an avalanche

subsides into   space

crashes down

the side of a mountain

at the end of an avenue

on a walk, makes itself heard

      as causal

the birds fly

at Vespers to the bells

fresh from cedar and moss-dabbed woods

framing the abbey, arcing to embrace

fields of red tiled roofs, the sound

audible: visible   visceral

for miles round—

the call to holiness
seen and felt

going to chapel, a monk

the hall is as it was before: noiseless

even though he walks to purpose

in soft-soled black leather shoes

a thousand years before; brown robes

obscure

the sample of humanity given to

poverty, chastity, obedience: the monk

arrives to chapel at end of another 1,000 years;

today showing, how it was, is and shall be—

    (in the main) unchanged

standing image

there is a tree made of iron

with browning leaves, dropping
onto glass tabletops

its branches flaming out
to touch

heads nodding

by half

I wake, without the alarm

red numbers sketched in dark space

stalking streets

lining dreams not quite

half-remembered, still hidden

in shadows — signals of clocks, hours

blink in conjunction with the world I

must soon rejoin, but

not yet mine (the lights murky)

      sleep an ally

Jordan River

clean

like a god, to roam

penniless in deserts where

money is everything—

you dip your body, surrender

to live free of all that might confine

a prophet from speaking

a better word for a better

god—God in place of all

we might otherwise

believe

drink

how you thirst

dryness, a curse

so long without water — how long

        has it been

you reach for my glass: water

I let it go, freely, but it will not

fill you up, I fear

how you thirst

to take the veil

desire God; echo the sacrifice

the timeless need

to turn away

enter something solid,

less obscure

than obscurity in the eyes

of the world

the world deeply loved —

and, so prayed for

this is what it means, to kneel

at the altar: to affirm, fulfill

self-denial

we might trust

the dam has broken, a wall
around living trees, against nature

branches obey the force, snap in the flood

limbs torn from trunks form
improbable rafts —

　　　remain buoyant

derailed

we wander   mid-day

luggage thrown
from the train, still running
    through our mind

    people
decoupled

    searching for a moment before
    the crash

sifting through

unshed tears

a type of sanctuary, conspiracy

for souls too strong to cry   out loud

squeeze through small shafts, openings between words,

teachings shrinking, expanding, becoming

      something else,

something personal, very personal

      small

not wanting to give the wrong impression

or appear awkward

tears remain tight, locked up

to swell and prevent

the soul from losing its place in line,

its ability to contribute, lend its power

      become small

squeeze through the shaft opening

      to release power

shimmering

where are the hills I can run to?

does the track leading upwards

begin here at the crossroads, somewhere between errands

and dreams become legend, now fact?

when did my spirit grow crowded? confused?

my eyesight slightly off centre; my skin like thoughts

less alert

where are the hills I can run to for more from my Maker;

the one who knows the way from here; I am here,

but where is the track that leads upwards

now, in this moment

where are —   the hills?

one third rational

your soul commands your body

to work; sweep the floor

to eat   follow through

work to eat

even as tears fill bottles in heaven —

their salty substance

real enough to touch,

to taste

they do the work you need

to eat

to find peace

collect your thoughts in the morning, first—

give them to God, who is half-part of anything we give

and could be more, like dawn first-light-giving

rise to the fullness of day, and all time

minutes into hours; more

than we realize

by grace

the definition of arrival is when

you realize

how far you've come

solace

the dream of success can interfere

with a good night's sleep

but it helps to get alone in the woods

and listen to the sound of my heart

to hear: how faith (and even fear)

outweigh   man's accolades

how much more important: the sound

of my heart alone in the woods

Postcard

let his peace settle

     reflect his glory

like mountains in a moraine lake

on a clear day

the goodness of God

held level with earth

an image, waited upon,

multiplies

evergreen

independent.

individual.

attuned to the voice of God

leading on from glory to glory, higher

deeper, more assured

guilt-free

and able —

to obey in love

red, yellow, blue

three umbrellas keeping out rain

offer shelter; set expectations — refuge

in smart talk or close friendship; the third

a cover for family relations, spiritual banners

all three, serving their own

P.S.

keep no secrets

beneath boulders, hidden

on roads dedicated to openness

salt

to live the rest of my life in the shadow

of a building determined to be tall

is not my idea of living

I want to walk with Gandhi

to the sea —

to do something simple

Adam

my friend is afraid he's becoming a cynic (afraid of saying he's disappointed);

he's beginning to see through pretense, spotting hidden agendas;

the only thing hidden from him

is God

and so, he's afraid

a few words

tell me more

in a few words

      tears, laughter

about angels' wings, forgiveness over

lunch, quiche and coffee —

finding when we're heard (when we speak)

there is someone waiting there

to journey   all the way

we've come

to become human

wrecked forever as a creature of the deep

our words signal floundering, a losing of the way

to find, unsound in silence, the need to speak

become human

something other than —

revolution

we live closer to the sun in September

when it snows; and tell each other truths

to keep the world turning   young ones

your mother doesn't really believe

flicker

the flame is weak, but taken as life

to the breast of the woman

chilled at the hearth

of gathered coal

now cooling

mountains

metaphors

for age, weight and other obstacles

    to overcome

    in time

appearance

there you were! on my birthday — a surprise
to help me get on, to fill the gaps between years

you laughed and presented a stunning purple scarf,
embellished with silver elephants — superfluous

something about them not representing anything
      other than

the affection of a friend, a hug saying
      you are real
            all is well

a running theme

the freefall between calls —

me calling you when you don't
call me

a fracture line threatens, upholds
the only narrative we have
between us

and I wonder why I fear the end,
calling it quits
instead

of calling you —

you seem upset, my friend

the last time we talked I heard something in your voice

suggesting all might not be well, but, between us, if

you're upset and dissatisfied, then let me offer

you a place—permission—to go and forget,

to leave there, in that place, all I did or failed to do

for you—where I have fallen short, forget—

and I will too

paper cuts

the mailbox was the same: letters came

carrying enough to smash the child's world

in half, divorce papers   paper cuts

they said they were resilient

would adjust   form new alliances

with adult love, words

         only words, names

           on paper

deaf to hearing

understand

    we diverge

sunshine through curtains, belonging

to different suns, words (elements of conversation)

colliding, failing

to bridge

the span

saving for a rainy day

anyone who learns to breath under water

might make it through

in a flood, don't

you think?

truth

written in stone, like walls built around a city

or meteors shaped in the atmosphere

to house and inhabit

the void

can companion the strongest defenders,

comfort the weak

transform

indiscernible endings

the adventure shifts from out there

to in-here, home for the night

with a big bowl of popcorn

and a blanket, with you,

to watch a foreign

film about all

there is to

life

unburdened

suddenly, you speak

fill my soul with your voice

     and here, we overlap in the space

     away from officialdom,

     brought home,

     approved

     as linguists

twin hopes

heading north, to find some peace and quiet,

shut out the noise; get away from it all —

        perhaps, write home

        with news of all

        I've found

patterns repeat

flowers (bright, orange-red) and fruit (mangoes):

          failed to sell before best-before

found in the dumpster by a bird in the form of a man

gray, discarded behind the depot, seed better off

in the earth, replenishing supply —

he thought, like a sun

bright, orange-red

the (professor's) talking stick

use words to make yourself heard, speak up
say what you mean, and mean it

easy, right?

everyone has a voice, unless they don't
and even then, there are ways

to be understood

what could be simpler? what could be—

simpler?

charm offensive

glossy mares
    stampede

tear up dust

in the face of what can only be
    fear, instinct
    drive

for peace: stampede
turn up dust
storm

words rarely do the trick

reflecting back now

memory deepens with age, or falls apart —
it could go either way

making for a beautiful last chapter to life, or a rough one

we'll remember something, a little or a lot
of a kiss, the hand on our back, pressing,
telling us we are not alone

how much we recall, growing —

leaks

like water

anger can seep through

the foundation, break pipes,

overturn roots, taint soil

defy the insurance plan

small impressions

2 coppers in the snow

leave their mark

there to melt

wanting you

time finds me
impatient, standing
at the bank today and tomorrow
downtown having coffee
with you, but let's not talk
about what we have (or lack);

let's take the hour to say
what we feel — okay?

given a day

If you only have a day, call me if you can.

No pressure, but I'd love to hear from you;

but… if you only have a day

and choose to write or paint instead,

I'll understand.

Perhaps we'll see each other on a walk by the river

where we go to be alone: and we'll be glad.

We can always catch up later, unless you only have a day,

but then I'll understand.

hay bales

the pottery class

take a piece of clay,

give shape to what might be,

add air, push — this way and that —

coax raw material with water, motion, skill

rotate the lump, draw forth beauty

let your hands do the work,

rest your mind, rely

on being a potter

at the wheel

learn how love makes sure —

how art

acts

on senses loosed

spinning hope

from clay

shy, yet firm

science shows

the dipper in the sky I learned as a child

as a constellation hanging true

to the storybook image

lying mute, 2D

on a page

isn't quite right —

the stars, I learn as I unlearn, live apart

from each other, spaced out in every

direction, far from the flat

surface I named and

called my own

the universe goes on and on, full-bodied

inexplicable beauty

causing me to wonder still more what more

there might be showing

      this side of heaven

trending

art has been erased from the café; its white walls

embody the blank notion that thought,

left to itself, might ennoble the air

as people talk and drink

and try to relate

without art

Bistro

in the restaurant

on the most popular night of the week

talk is   a ride at the waterpark

we drop through, survive

silence a long way off, why did we come

the gomaae, exquisite,

plated   a portal

to indulge another

sensibility   drop through

survive

My Aunt's House

at the start of the stairs winding up

I see a photo of a woman with a face like my own, a marker

       I am close to home

even if the stories are forever under construction —

and barely hold me in, like this house

out of time, I listen for —

saws, hammers,

voices

what to make of the photos on the walls, some

faded, some new, some missing —

voices

reconstructing what it means to live, close to home

but not all in the same house, hearing

the same stories

told

hay bales

prairie icons dot the landscape between

Edmonton and Red Deer

places with names on the map

held together with smaller ones

like Ponoka and Wetaskiwin

where cars are cheaper and the rodeo

happens once a year, on Canada Day,

when the stands come alive

with people off the QE2

come to pay to see young men

dance with horses, rope calves

far from the city, close to the heart

of the country grandfathers

built for days like these

ahead of their time

farmers, first-generation

passing on

icons

boxed noodles

the children eat their meal-on-the-go

in the jammed food court

the week before school,

bags crammed

mom on her phone, detached

the children eat, absorb

small town café

did you know, potholes, the mayor (20 years uncontested)

leases left gaping/closed; billboards for small business

vanilla 1% lattes, cookies that are delicious

(car pools: arranged) and we'll see you

tomorrow, back here

debris

good-will boats scoop out clogs in the ocean

battling to breath: filter through

bewildering trade-off's

with good-will

nursing home (night shift)

her mother couldn't get warm — flannels, soft winter duvet,

the heat cranked up, oppressive to someone hitting (hitting!)

menopause, doing her best to take care of the other — the

other part of her soul joined in the hymn they sang the night

her mother couldn't get warm   love a sacred duty

      finding its way down the long hall,

      come to relieve her...

      keep her mother warm

Intersections

heading North on 149th

the train

criss-crossed my path,

diverting me to the right —

    down the Yellowhead

not for the first time

my path at 90-degree angles

    to my plans

more than once have I headed North

    only to turn East

and found the wind (pleasantly) at my back —

FROM THE AUTHOR

I hope you enjoyed this grouping of spiritual poems, relational soundings and thoughtful observations.

the birds fly is my 5th collection.

My poetry has been published in *Crux, Weavings, Alive Now, Presence Journal, Transition Mental Health Journal, The Prairie Messenger, Prairie Journal* and *Island Writer*.

My background is a mix of journalism, philosophy and theology. I'm an author, poet and speaker, with friends who listen well and lend joy and strength to the writing journey.

I currently live in Edmonton, Alberta with my family.

www.daynawrites.com

Dayna E. Mazzuca

Made in the USA
Lexington, KY
07 June 2019